Aerial View of Louisiana

for Robert Pack,
with best wishes -
Cleopatra Mathi

AERIAL VIEW OF LOUISIANA

poems by

Cleopatra Mathis

The Sheep Meadow Press
New York City

ACKNOWLEDGMENTS

American Poetry Review: "For Maria," Grandmother," "Los Americanos," "Riding on Empty." *The Ardis Anthology of New American Poetry:* "Rearranging My Body," "Two Memories." *Columbia:* "Journey in the Snow Season." *City:* "Her Letter." *The Denver Quarterly:* "Family Life," "Finding the Quarry," "Ruston, La.: 1952," "Snow." *The Georgia Review:* "Mimosa." *Gilt Edge:* "The Lost Woman." *Green River Review:* "Learning to Live with Friends." *Intro 9:* "Inventing Ourselves. *The Nation:* "Padre Island." *The New England Review:* "Aunt Drucilla's Pasture." *The New Yorker:* "Getting Out." *Pequod:* "A Place of Another Name," "The Ghosts of the Animals," "As You Stalk the Sleep of My Forgetting." *Ploughshares:* "The Traveler," "Stars in Water." *Plum:* "For My Sister," "After the Funeral." *Poetry Now:* "Peaches: For My Mother." *The Seattle Review:* "Conversation in Winter," "The Trees." *The Southern Review:* "The Bats," "Bittersweet Nightshade," "For Allison, On the Obscenity of Flowers," "Making Bread for the Dying in the Next House." *Stockpot:* "Celebrating the Mass of Christian Burial." *Traveling America With Today's Poets:* "Aerial View of Louisiana," "Pine Barrens: Letter Home." *Virginia Quarterly Review:* "The Gift."

Acknowledgment is also made to U.S.I. Poets Cooperative. I would like to thank the friends who have given me their encouragement and support. I am especially grateful to Stanley Kunitz, Daniel Halpern, Stanley Plumly, and Bill Mathis.

Published by The Sheep Meadow Press
New York, New York
Cover design by Jacques Hnizdovsky
Printed and manufactured in the United States
by The Studley Press, Dalton, Massachusetts
Distributed by Persea Books, Inc., 225 Lafayette Street,
New York 10012, New York

ISBN 0-935296-00-X (cloth); 0-935296-01-8 (paper)
Library of Congress Catalog Card Number 79-90841
First Printing

for Cleopatra Theodos
and Maxine Theodos Long

Contents

I. Padre Island: A Sanctuary

Padre Island 3
The Gift 4
The Trees 5
Learning to Live With Friends 6
Getting Out 7
Making Bread for the Dying in the Next House 8
Celebrating the Mass of Christian Burial 9
Finding the Quarry 10
Rearranging My Body 11
For My Sister 12
As You Stalk the Sleep of My Forgetting 14

II. Aerial View of Louisiana

Aerial View of Louisiana 17
A Place of Another Name 18
Grandmother 20
Two Memories 22
Ruston, La.: 1952 23
For Maria 24
Family Life 25
House of Animals 26
The Traveler 27
Mimosa 28
Souvenir 29
Pine Barrens: Letter Home 32

III. Inventing Ourselves

Bittersweet Nightshade 37
Inventing Ourselves 39
Los Americanos 40
The Lost Woman 41
Riding on Empty 42
For Allison, On the Obscenity of Flowers 43
Her Letter 44
The Bats 45
After the Funeral 46
Two Poems from Grimm: Silver Hands 47
                        The Six Swans 49
Stars in Water 50
Conversation in Winter 51
Meditation on Crete 52

IV. For Bill

Your Mother Takes Us Back to Liberty 57
You Go Home, 1968 59
Aunt Drucilla's Pasture 61

V. In Another Life

In Another Life 65
Bees 66
Delta House 67
Peaches: For My Mother 69
Snow 71
Foreigner 72
Journey in the Snow Season 74
The Animals Choose Their Path into My Sleep 76

I. Padre Island: A Sanctuary

Padre Island

You could be lonely here
forever, that sanctuary of cries
something to live for, the smell of dying
sea life almost loving.
Nothing that lives wild
asks for mercy, the silent fish,
the sacrifice of birds.
                    You'd never stop seeing
through that water. Consider the branches
and limbs around your face, the obscuring
moon, how you fight each loss.
You'd clear yourself
here, limited to the flat
open white, egret and pelican
taking their innocent food. Nothing's permanent
but this, the unbroken
cartilage of fish reappearing.

Compare your inadequate spine,
its frail anger, the empty arch
of your foot seeking strength. The skin,
a delicate memory whose recital of cold
you never forget. Think how you've been changed,
debts your body can't overcome, the humor
of your devotion. Here, the ocean owns itself,
wild geese mate for life. And you, trying
to make yourself necessary,
while around you the birds
answer their true and final lives.

The Gift

Because of your age, your stiffening body,
they make x-rays of the child
at eight months. It is male
with fine silk hairs. Against your stretched
translucent skin, they hear his raspy breath,
the heartbeat. I have no child
but have placed the cat purring
against my stomach in the dark.
I imagine the insistent paw of a child's kick.
Curled around that motion, I sleep,
concave, firm as a boy.

I am making your child
a horse of pine and oak, a mane
from my braided hair. With the finest tools
I perfect the hollow wood,
the tiny saddle sewn from calf.
Nights I hear rocking in the deep part
of the house. You cannot sleep
for that moving in the womb's heart.
Already the baby tries to cry,
hums as he rocks, rides
back and forth in the dark.

The Trees

His room was small, filled
with windows. Outside, the ripe trees
full of green fruit. He wanted only to sleep
but slept lightly, waking with a dream
like a painting, a frail landscape
of birds in some trees, lovely
without leaves. He composed another scene:
his long years, stiff with decisions,
a landscape of failure, and closed his eyes
against it, remembering how he once covered
young trees with burlap against the ice.
Then turned away finally to sleep
thinking: our bones are filled
with a dust that is obedient
and poisonous. When the body calls them
to move, the bones gather the flesh
tightly around their pale branches
but their strength is the soul's
black dust calling.

Learning to Live With Friends

Like you, your house had a beauty
that rules its surroundings,
modifies itself. The ownership was clear—
you had no use for curtains, the shutters
never closed. At night, wood floors
gleamed after you. Wherever I walked
I was not alone. By day, all that white:
light gave the walls everything you wanted.
Plants breathed like children.

Up by six in the haze, we drank coffee
for hours, watered porch baskets of fuschia.
Around us, the country loaned a solitude,
our bodies darkened. I thought how warm you looked,
sulking in a blue shirt. Later you brought out anger
and I saw that heat was old in you.

Caroline, I have seen some of your skins,
the layered dark and light that contain you
like a cloud. In a rage, you wore yourself.
Those storms left us nowhere to hide;
you claimed the rooms you screamed in,
husband following. I don't know what he offered,
perhaps some care that marriage lends.
I'm writing this because I had nothing to give
except the fear friends have.
I saw some madness in you like my own,
the kind we speak of but rarely show.
That boundary is its own pain. I watched you
as I watch myself.
Seeing us both, I turned away.

Getting Out

That year we hardly slept, waking like inmates
who beat the walls. Every night
another refusal, the silent work
of tightening the heart.
Exhausted, we gave up; escaped
to the apartment pool, swimming those laps
until the first light relieved us.

Days were different: FM and full-blast
blues, hours of guitar "you gonna miss me
when I'm gone." Think how you tried
to pack up and go, for weeks stumbling
over piles of clothing, the unstrung tennis rackets.
Finally locked into blame, we paced
that short hall, heaving words like furniture.

I have the last unshredded pictures
of our matching eyes and hair. We've kept
to separate sides of the map,
still I'm startled by men who look like you.
And in the yearly letter, you're sure to say
you're happy now. Yet I think of the lawyer's bewilderment
when we cried, the last day. Taking hands
we walked apart, until our arms stretched
between us. We held on tight, and let go.

Making Bread for the Dying in the Next House

I collect ingredients for the bread.
I dissolve old honey
into the yeast, take salt
from the husband you can't remember,
already a lifetime in the ground.
As I knead, lightning
takes your son again, your daughter
lies back down. Eight cups of flour
for the lost. You are dry and milky,
still flowing into the dead
who know us by our insistent hands.

I make a fist and punch down the dough.
I pound the bread
but your death won't stop. It buries itself,
it swells. I have the grief
of the living, the worrisome mother
of flesh, its demands.
You release yourself
deep into the bread.

I shape the small bodies of dough,
arrange them in tins,
cover them with linen.
You are silent, having closed your eyes
with comfort. The bread rises
and the whole cloth of your life
burns away. You grow remote
with the privacy of death,
approaching another place
to abide without body,
without hunger.

Celebrating the Mass of Christian Burial

Anna Barry, 1883-1977

The air changes, blooms.
The geranium in your room across the yard
is blank as the chair. March has come —
the clouds swell and break, lifting the sky
out of gray. Last month you promised
this clearness loosening the dogwood.

I can see past your house and mine,
past the road that borders
the canal, a child of the river. Water collides,
creates reflection. I recognize
a different landscape, the detail of black
and red lace on the river, the small sun
through the trees.

This kind of sight is transient,
I know it won't be the same again.
Three days ago, you held a clear glass
of sherry and willed a change.
The removal of ourselves is like this,
the quick fog of our lives
rising past the boundaries we know, past the season
of our own deaths.

Finding the Quarry

for Bill

Surrounding rock, the firs and open forest.
Another life we've come to, a clearing
in the hills of the mountain. White rock
on three sides, the sudden drop off that ledge.
On the bottom, a small birch growing
over stone, its cluster of leaves
beginning to turn. How many died here—
more under us than rock: bones, fool's gold,
quartz given up by miners. Our footprints filled
with water, the steady drip
escaping rock, a tiny song the quarry carries.
We stayed awhile, at ease in that graveyard,
thinking of change. Still it brought back a past
and that pain of extremes, our own cliffs
and the rock-ribbed tree of yellow leaves.

Rearranging My Body

I have a woman's feel for time,
hands that know when to be innocent.
When you watch me, I am graceful
like any southern girl
who learned to yield, easily
borrowed the rhythms of walking.
Black women washed my skin
and showed me when to leave well enough alone.

Now this changes: my mouth widens.
I am wild with hair. I strip
off this cotton dress, tear apart
my legs that will learn their own time.
I reach inside,
my stomach becomes a new fist,
I rearrange the obedient fingers of my ribs.

You'll see my body,
the new hard curves
of a woman bent over in a soybean field.
You'll smell the overcooked greens,
the brown sweat. Even now, see my wrist,
the underside thin and pale
as a fish's belly, the veins
strong as catgut.
I am no longer familiar. It is all right
if you never want me again.

For My Sister

You wouldn't cry, not even with the glass
in your foot: a mirror broken in the water,
those silver fragments finer than other glass.
You came out without a word, wrapped it
with whatever would hold the blood.
The ragged flaps of flesh turned white,
the fish on the bank beside you
opened and closed the fans of their gills.

Still far away I reach to understand that parish
you never leave. You pile the damp towels
on the sickroom floor. Your lover
closed into fever, into quarantine
in the foggy house, tells you again
about the tiny fish swimming in his lungs,
how they settle like gold coins, bright spots
of water flickering so he can't sleep.
He wants to cough them up. Delirium
is part of the disease, you say,
expecting more blood.

The water off the dock was cloudy
from swamp moss, rotted cypress full of nails.
None of us waded there. And when you stepped in,
you must have seen the broken glass reflecting
in the water. You made your familiar short sound,
almost a gasp, as if the water felt a little cold,
then calmly walked your way out of there.

You are always smaller than I remember,
thinner than those water reeds I loved to pick
and gather to my own side of the room.
You are far away, my dark fish.
Broken lung, heart's crystal:
I would hold you if I could.

As You Stalk The Sleep of My Forgetting

Again I walk into the cluster of bayou trees,
the gray bark stripped by deer.
This far south, winter repeats itself
in rain, keeps the land half marsh.
You are hunting, quail at your belt,
covered by the chatter of birds
and small game. Again I try to guess
your exact place in the pine
and cypress, avoid your steps,
the aim of your gun.

Later you'll hide yourself
in those I trust: this man, that woman.
Always I am called back to you.
By now I have lifted heavily
my body's dark sleep, and I know
it is not that other house.
You are not doing your Indian walk
into my room, where I hold my body
tight against my breasts,
body wrapped in wool.

You can no longer touch me.
Still I stalk that land
where I will find the safe bodies you have taken.
And I must finally hold the knife
against their throats, must uncover you
in those ragged trees, and fight myself awake
into this northern cold,
the house secure in snow
that is still falling.

II. Aerial View of Louisiana

Aerial View of Louisiana

The delta lies unchanged, flat
as childhood: a woman gathering pecans
from a yard black with water, purple martins
after mosquitoes, all winter mock lilac.

In the dream of wrought iron
you find them — the grandmother is fierce,
both arms waving you away. Your mother
takes your hand to speak
of fishing from low pine flats,
how she loves the nests of water.
She says your pride will be her death.
You wear your grandmother's wild name,
her fan of hair.

You wake to mountains: reflections
off coastal islands, hills of prairie marsh.
Memory is the first claim,
you'll spend your life coming back
to this flatness. By dusk you have forgotten
everything but the bleeding outline
of the river. You watch for New Orleans,
the white cluster of tombs.

A Place of Another Name

I speak from this location, the present
where I wake with a rosary of names
in a place without fig or mimosa.
A forest is collecting here,
straight as bone that forms the dead
even when the dead are gone. Around me
the hours fall into themselves.
I wear another history, a box of flesh
is how I keep it.

I am surrounded by those who know
their descent, who bring back generations
of names. My veins are muddy,
gold-brown, willed by my grandmother
with olives from Mitiline. She gave me
the name never given, won't let me forget
my obligation. I carry her in my clothes;
she wraps me, a garment sewn with stones.

But she is bones away in another skin,
a place of another name. I drag myself
into the frame of the present.
My heart winds itself daily, I need the calm
of lead. I consider the rock passage
to a water where birds fly low
and lighter, lifting their wings.

I say this into the mouth of the future
with its vacant measure of time, past memory
that holds us to names. From marrow of edgebone
to white .moon of nail, I am tenuous,
claimed by the touch of faces,
hands loose as rain. In this life
I learn to stay north, I search
a way to go. All the days end as water.

Grandmother (1895-1925)

When her father said she was a fool
to go with the white man, she only smiled,
thinking how his eyes were blue in the foxglove
and turned away to hide her face.

She wasn't frightened, the journey down the Ouachita
at flood stage, the spring swelling.
She showed him the golden raintree raining
gold buds, how to pound filo,
strip cane. She gathered aniseed, split alevara

for the time of the child
who stretched inside, but never told,
practiced in a squat. At night they lay belly to back,
the baby thrust its weight against him.

For twelve seasons of the river rising,
babies cried in the black wood cabin.
She made them shifts of calico and darning string.
He brought her flowers from the milkwort,
long reeds. He loaded river mud and carp,
planted collards on the banking slope.
They lived the Choctaw way,
apart from others like flint arrows.

The fourteenth year, she tended their needs
the same. Winter shoved into April,
they kept the windows stuffed with paper.
At the time of birth she sent him out;
for years he blamed himself: a betrayal
of the blood he joined. And when he died
he saw her by the bed, the infant
in her arms, her hair soaked red.

Two Memories

Did you exist, ever?
Did I ride on your shoulders,
did you rock me as I slept?
I know you were tall and carried the weight
of three wives. And though you left us,
your blood is mine.

I have been given this memory.
The cabin where your father lived, leaning wood
on the high bank of the Mississippi.
The slope rotting into water.
Inside, two rooms divided by fireplace
for heat, mantel burdened with bibles
and faded pictures of thirteen children.
He was a godly man, my mother says,
who took a Cherokee wife.

I remember the smell of darkness,
remember my sleep
with animals under the handmade floor,
the stone foundation grunting and the wind
finding the spaces between the boards.
You were there, but I see my grandfather.
And though I open the memory wider,
your face and body merge gently into his.
He is pouring molasses
the color of the winter river on a plate
of biscuits, and the cold
stands stiff inside me.

Ruston, La.: 1952

The man plays harmonica
stomping around the kitchen
and the sound of Oh Susanna wakes the child.
Here is the woman walking her children
before dawn, the clacking of the stroller
down the empty streets of the town.

Years leave us but the real snow
is still in the picture, the small girl
with socks on her hands
smiling thigh-deep in snow. You leave us for good
but I face the blackboard easel,
my chalk letters.
This is the picture of the girl turning her back
when the father says goodbye.

Every year a small child in me
grows larger, surrounded by the ribs of the past.
She rearranges the chronicle of pictures.
The years behind us become smaller,
clearer, as in an engraving
or the trees on a familiar street, repeating
and repeating.

For Maria

The hot nights I slept with you,
a leg thrown across your back.
You never complained.
When our stepfather raved, I fought.
You didn't cry with me,
preferring the dog and grassy field.
I thought you lived in your own world.
Now what I know best about you
comes from that night at supper in the hot kitchen.
You clenched your teeth as long as you could
against his slash of belt
on my bare foot. But when the blood came
you screamed in my place, Bastard, bastard!
and stopped us all.

Later in bed we heard the words of our stepfather
through the wall, the breaking of our mother
who couldn't come to us if we called.
Next to the window, you faced the ledge;
the honeysuckle told lies
as you put out your hand, all night
held the small flowers.

Family Life

When you came, you took the house
from us, that shouting
and that rack of guns
driving us out. I can't count the pranks
you pulled with the cunning
of a crazy man, the phones unwired
when you were gone, the night you broke every dish
and piled them in the cabinets.

Or those blanks you loaded.
Waiting by the kitchen door, shotgun
across your knees, you picked us off
one by one, as we came in from school.
Maria's big eyes and your own son
screaming. An hour of that, then mother
came home, fried some rabbit
and we all sat down to eat.

House of Animals

Here are the closed-up rooms of childhood,
the stiff possessions: deerheads
of a stepfather, our mother's mounted squirrel.
I find the ghosts of every stray
taken in, the cat without a voice, the biting dog.
Hungry, they surrounded us in such little space.
My brother still lives in that odd collection
of flesh. He nails more guns to the wall.

I'm collecting the useless animals
of the past, putting the crippled to rest.
Here are my brother's first tools
to get even: clothes pins and BB gun,
lost kittens of my snowball cat.
Back to back, we recede into that country
of aliens. He's ten again, and the old man,
stringing rabbits, laughs at his limp.
Saturday morning, he's skinny in bed, can't move
his legs. It's not my fault, I scream, get up—
you *got* to get up, and I beat his white stiff legs.

My brother keeps his room the same
as prayer, keeps that smile our language.
Jimmy, take your hand from the animals,
now empty as dolls. Put back each weapon
we used to blame, every fear we have owned.
We'll turn our backs and leave that house.

The Traveler

It's raining like the day you walked out,
harmonica in your pocket, the suitcase of shirts.
I'm thinking of you again, with your variety
of wives: the cajun, my mother the Greek,
and Alberta the Texas peach.
Reminded by this dull rain and every man I see
absently touching his child, of how you smiled
and left, never sent letters or money.
Consider your ten years to make it back
just that once. My blond-ringleted picture
yellowing inside your wallet. You were so charming,
at ease. To forget, I sliced the length of every finger
with a gillette blade. Now the next wife writes:
you want to be a father. Daddy,
here is my reply, filled with your debts.
You left blood behind, that permanent traveler
thickening our lives. Do you know
how long it outlasts hate,
love; do you know how long?

Mimosa

After twenty-five years they drag you away.
Nothing left but roots and this wish
To know that you recognized us, the living
Who still come back, the dead who wear the white
Blur of themselves.

The children crying into summer—
We must have seemed hopeless, every unhappiness
Taken to the highest branch,
Our swearing to leave. Remember the dark blue
St. Augustine grass, the roses.

Go back as far as the old man
On his haunches blowing smoke rings. Suspenders,
Long underwear, the handpainted
Delicate cup of thick coffee.
You have been planted an hour.
See the pack of Camels in the grass, the little girl.
She frames the scene
As through glass, which will thicken
And distort, until the man has faded
Into distance. And you and the child
Have moved through years, changed
And disappeared.

Souvenir

1.

This one's of you, standing on the beach
in your black bathing suit. Inside the rectangular eye
of the plastic viewer, you are lovely,
brown as a girl, your shadow
a dark place on the sand. One elbow is slightly bent,
underneath the drooping arc of skin
the arm's young curve not quite disguised.
You look half-amused,
as if you know the photographer
admires you. Summer after summer

you rubbed cantaloupe on my face
telling me you were so beautiful in 1922
that all the women talked and were shocked
when you took out your handkerchief in the heat
and no color rubbed away. All the melon,
rose-honey, I still didn't have skin like that.

You laugh when I want only the small souvenirs,
offering this time the picture of my grandfather
at seventeen in his three-cornered army hat.
You say by now it's locked in your mind.
Every year the house is more empty,
you've given so much away. I want to know
the stories I can't remember, the names
from the other language. But you won't talk
about the donkeys you rode up and down
the olive mountain, how you learned
to keep your legs from rubbing raw.

Or the Turks who took your family,
shot them one by one, even the baby brother.
It's possible to live too long
you tell me, you want nothing from memory.

2.

My dream is whiter than the glaring
backdrop of sand. You summon me,
having decided the time to die. The freezing landscape
is unfamiliar, a vacant house behind us.
Crying, I take your hand. You say this death
has nothing to do with me, you do not say goodbye.
The white air distracts me, a wide bird
glides along the glittering surface.
I look back: my hand is empty.

Now I have dreamed you dead
there is ice in my chest, a tiny lump
of terror. You have shown me your coffin
but I can't wash your body,
plug the holes. And the eyes, I won't
let them close. Or find the two gold pieces
you gave me when your husband died.
Your spirit has found my bed,
these nights I hold you safe
as the photograph in plastic,

YaYa, I breathe snow
when I look into this tiny picture,
hold it to the light. My lungs ache
in their blanket of cold.

It's winter here, and your warmth
so easily enclosed. I'm trapped outside
and need to talk. My Greek is not good enough,
I learned the practical. I swear you never taught
the heart-word, only kissed your fingertips
when you looked at me. It's the years between us
that take you away. Half a century
and the water makes ice. I can't get through.

No, I don't look like you.
My skin is marked, has always shown each eye's line
for tears. Still I peer into the scene of beach sand,
looking for resemblance.
You are the same, unreachable
in that viewer's square. You've given me
a framed icon, the bracelet of coins
and Greek charms, a bedspread you crocheted,
your mother's stained scarf, a christening diamond,
your gift for going on.

Pine Barrens: Letter Home

It could be Louisiana, attracting rain.
Soft ground, low land marshes
creeping into ragweed. These names own themselves.
Think of sassafras, a wildness never caught.

Rowing the sucking water
you said, look for the dead men, watch now,
three went over the dam last week.
Black Lake with the cajun ladies, noisy nights
you woke me for fishing. The snapshot of dark
Campti shows your wide hat, a crying child.

I think of the Blacks
who called at night, took you to their church,
baskets of beans we found on the porch.
I wouldn't touch your red snapper or stew.
But I've found crawfish in the pine barrens
of New Jersey, swamps bordered with ginger root.
And the people distrusting ties,
losing themselves the same.
Some recognition keeps after me:
I pulled away, now I can't forgive
my own survival. It's true I live apart
but like a root.

Your letters come asking for money,
catfish aren't biting, too much rain.
The garden swells with mud. The wide black walnut
crashed at Campti, lessons of moss collapsing
on Black Lake. Like other times, you'll manage.
I've searched you for blame, for anger.
If I could I'd drag back everything: husbands, sons,
years. But you say you love us all—
even departure is a sign
the return is certain.

III. Inventing Ourselves

Bittersweet Nightshade

for Stanley Kunitz

Late evening: the unstaked tomatoes,
the slugs waiting in the lettuce.
In the same month as my birth, another ending,
still with childhood closed in my palm.
I slip off shoes and walk away

to a house with bright windows. A man writes
at a table, at ease in the moment's arrangement.
It's the particular light that reminds me
of another yard with fig and walnut trees,
the same blocks of houselight
shaping the lawn. And I'm small again with bandaged knees
watching my grandfather dance. Wrists high,
he turns around the room. The slow dips to the floor
make his handkerchief's white shadow fly·
against the glass. There is no music
and he dances with himself. I watch
in the damp summer grass.

Or it's another night, the same life repeated.
I've been fighting again, and run out
on the street in the dark. Separation
seems a natural thing. I make the circle of houses
again and again on the silver-turned street
until the lights blink out on everybody's porch.
Then drag my hands through nightshade,
put them to my mouth. I swore I'd never go back.

I walk until the moon rises white.
Still the voyeur of lighted houses, the open rooms
at dusk. Still trying to walk out of the body
of my past, finally outside myself,
released. I go through the blurred animal shapes
of trees to my own yard, its familiar shadow.
I've waited years to go in, longing to see.
Now the moon off the window simply holds
the full oak. This house is empty, my house
is new. Each night I've walked out,
denying this.

Inventing Ourselves

Nights I rest against the shoulder
of sleep, your body that wraps me.
We sleep with the cold around us,
our mouths truthful and close as friends.

In the full current of night
we learn to be cruel to all that is deadly
in ourselves. We create distance
as if we were old and remembering
our bodies with kindness.

This is how we give names,
another blood, as though you had created
a child in the silk glove of my body.
The new child in the womb sleeps
with his mouth open, dreams
and dreams. Here is the tiny blue heart
of his imagination. It invents us
as we invent each other, tightening
a cord of solitude around us.

Los Americanos

In 1870, five hundred Southerners
left their homes to settle in Brazil.

After the war, we couldn't forget
our agreement with the dead
to never change. We spat in the dirt
when we spoke of the blacks, not for their absence,
but how they walked away
as though from dark bolls cleaned of cotton.
We dragged the fields,
our land; our women were brown
with work. And the children sobbing night after night,
their rooms empty of the smell
of slave women's moss beds.

We dug what silver we'd planted,
packed the loved ones' bones in boxes
and settled for likely climate. Brazil surrounded us
with jacaranda. Cane flourished
on cheap land; we kept our acres together,
kept our daughters for ourselves.
The drawls lengthened into Portuguese
but our names stay the same, our language keeps
the war and leaving. Every year polishing the stones
in the fenced graveyard, *Los Americanos,*
we keep alive.

The Lost Woman

As right as death in Calera, Alabama
the woman missed is mourned for. They found her
in cinquefoil on the roadside, curled like a child.
Dead, no longer owned by kidnapper
or parent, never identified in Birmingham.
Calera's people claimed her
from the mortuary; the sewing ladies dressed her
in lilac, washed her pale hair. First Baptist
collected for mums and the Bleeding Heart,
laid her out below the pulpit. To every man
she became a daughter, truer than his own,
or in that glow wore the look of his young wife
some twenty years ago. When they put her in the ground
even the school children said a prayer.
In the town's family cemetery
they keep her stone bare.

Riding on Empty

You were roughnecking off the coast,
right out of school with no place to go.
You came home grease-caked,
said it scared you to work the floor.
Mornings I opened the cafe at three,
where Mama was working her thirtieth year.
I cut the rows of pie and swore
every night to get out of there.
By August you had me down to my slip
and were saying you might make foreman.

Then one night at the Dixie
I heard my father's voice, a man I spoke of
as if he were dead. After fourteen years
he'd come back on a job, trying to fill D'Arbonne Swamp
in all that rain. I was half crazy
avoiding him, bone-tired in the heat,
tired of the haze, tired of the drizzle
that followed by night. Wherever I went
I thought I heard my father's voice.

The night I told you I was leaving for good,
all we had between us was a buck forty-nine
and your sweet Chevy. Riding on empty
all the way to Chenny Inn across the Ouachita line.
We parked with the six-pack, and no stars
showed over the old parish road.
You were too good to me that long night,
knew I meant only myself
when I talked about the danger of our bodies,
how they would let us down and hold us,
poor in that town for the rest of our lives.

For Allison, on the Obscenity of Flowers

I couldn't resist the armfuls that I gathered,
taking more and more, only because there were so many.
The kitchen was strewn with the dark
branches, the broken lilies of the valley.
Ankle-deep, I forced them into any container,
no jar or pitcher large enough. The blossoms dropped,
lovely in the litter of themselves,
whiter and thicker, more fragrant than I'd known
in the open air. Finally their insistence
made me faint. I began to lose breath
and imagined your entrance,
the line of your dark hair, your own whiteness
withdrawing: how you prefer the gift of one green pear.
And my bouquets an embarrassment about the room—
overwhelmed, you wouldn't speak; whole flowers
laced in my hair, against my waist. Jaded,
talkative, I was like some madam, growing heavier
with scent, overcome by the sadness of this world.
I saw it was best you were away
and it grieved me to protect you from my excess.
But as I made you perfect in thought,
you came and chose one stem with five blooms,
saying: every blossom is different,
yet each petal is formed the same.
My friend, we are so much alike.

Her Letter

For you I am sending an iron cross
begonia, the blooms already like clusters
of dried moths. I would have preferred black
walnuts from our old yard, their blandness
gives back so much, your wild taste for honey.
My days are calm, the blue light by my bed;
the little nurse makes a guard for the sun
in the window. I watch that division of light;
her greedy face reminds me of your new wife.
You think you'll give her what she wants.
I remember you best in fear, holding yourself
as you backed down the path. I wanted to tell you
about the children's feet powdered with dust,
the sun on their gold heads. How sweetly
they released their breath
when I laid them on the path to sleep.
They never felt the warm blade, and hardly bled.
For them I cut my hair against the scalp:
they would have left me too. Call me crazy,
sane; there are other reasons. Now I wear this
cotton blouse the way you'd like it,
my breasts still full of milk. When I walk
the concrete yard, I hold that baby flesh
again, and in your new life, you do not forget.

The Bats

My heart dreams of wings,
it beats like tympani.
It flies into itself, blind
and fixed in its white hole.

I open the door and let in the bats,
feathery and delicate
with disguise, limb given over to web,
the impulse of the dark.
They veer between the walls
all night and hang in the eaves,
they reverse themselves like dreams
in my dark house, vibrate
the thin membrane of my sleep.

Today a red spot thumps
on the artery of my wrist.
The bats are silver-haired
and light, furious
against the wall. They pound
and search with their radar of screams.
Mouths open like wounds,
they pulse at my feet, collapsing
their soft wings, hearts
not constrained by bone.

After the Funeral

Dirt-dauber nest in the kitchen
And the stuffed birds smell.
Mama's crying and stays in bed.
Brother, sister,
Nothing can live in this house.
Strip off the stoney apples
And throw them in the grass.
Bring cypress sticks, tear down mimosa,
Take the fallen flower stars.

But Mama won't stop crying.
She hears a whisper in the scattered camellias,
Empty-roofed pecans.
We are caught in the swollen web,
Roots of broken-down trees.
Brother sweats to cut them,
Sister boils them for tea.
Mama drinks it with lemon,
Blanket of branches over her bed.

Now she's up again
Limping in her flowered robe.
Black smell grows in the walls,
Roaches in the towels.
Tree stump, broken house,
Nothing will cover you.

Two Poems from Grimm

Silver Hands

In those days my right hand always cold,
the left unmatched, prophetic and white.
My father's eye gleamed,
he passed his left hand into the right
when he spoke. As I swept the yard I heard him
promise whatever stood under the trees
in exchange for coins and land. A dark wind
passed through; my left hand trembled,
the right one ice. I washed clean
and drew a circle round myself with chalk.
In a rage, the devil swore to take my hands.
I washed them with tears,
he could not pass over water. Father cried
my forgiveness, cried on my hands.
He cut them off to keep his life.
Then said: let me care for you with my new wealth.
I saw I understood nothing of men,
their lives bound to choice and possession.
Arms bound to my chest, I walked into a wood
where the trees are alike, unmarked.

I wandered days until the recovery
of gold-dark water. The glimmer of my body
submerged, the open veins freed from pain,
their dress of blood. I was carried
lighter than the swans across the circling moat
to an island cultivated with trees.
Dark, they reached over a dark horizon,
their fruit all I wanted, each perfect pear
counted on its limb. I put my mouth to one
and ate, only one, from its tree.

He gave me silver hands
and dressed me in silk. Claimed from his trees
in exchange for his pear. Angel of suffering,
my angel, he said and cried on my stumped wrists.
My soul emptied, I could not speak.
I shimmer with his gold, the measure
of possession, that kingdom. I am blessed,
weighed by these useless silver hands.
And of all I know in this world,
I prefer the single yellow pear and the water
that is bronze as the eye of the black swan.

The Six Swans

I hid when the woman brought her knotted feathers.
She gave my brothers wings, white breath
of swans. They blew on one another
when they found me and as a cloth is lifted,
so were their feathers stripped away.
The choice: scatter myself in grief or keep silent
to free them, weaving starwort and sea anemones,
my hands broken in the gathering.
Six years: I chose my bleeding hands,
fiery needles of the fabric.

Then discovery by the king, who swore to have me.
I threw down from the tree
as in madness, my ring, my apron, my skirt
to keep the vow. Determined, he took me
with his seed, the child I'd carry. In his house
I dreamed of a flock of birds, their wings
clipped at the elbow, hung in the stillness
of frost. I worked enclosed in that warning,
the air around me beat with wings.

Now each pierce of flesh gives sight
for dumbness: not even the killing of my child
will make me speak, my mouth sealed with blood.
Again this scene appears: the last day
when my brothers will surround me in the fire,
take their shapes as I throw out the shirts.
Then for my labor, every dark thread of pain,
still the youngest will bear like a whip,
one permanent white wing.

Stars in Water

We were walking through the shadows
of the Adirondacks. I saw so clearly
that unfamiliar country, our sudden friendship.
You said it couldn't be that way again,
walking that field, the small hands of birch leaves
fluttering in the still line of sunset.

The one night without a moon
seems now the end of summer. We walked
down the narrow road to the pond,
apart even from that separate world.
Sky floated over water,
a crowd of lights gleamed on black.
You said some of those stars
had already burned themselves out,
yet still they lived on the glass surface
of the pond. And I thought, even this landscape
is accidental.

On the last day the weather changed.
We walked past pond and field,
watched the stream mirror the cloudy sky,
variations of sun turning in the water.
The movement of light and shadow changed the rocks
as if by years. We left unexplained
whatever changes in ourselves
and walked back to our deliberate lives.

Conversation in Winter

In this season everything changes,
our bodies taking in the cold, a mask
of failure. Again some secret winter
stiffens every promise, the best intentions
laid down like your blue teapot
from another country. You and I speak
into the inexact mirrors of our cups:
cancellations to get through, the screaming
practices of bad days. Another search
into the grief of the mad women, oven-breathers,
little dreamers of death. It's unmistakable,
the reason for all this cold, how it grips
the changes you keep trying to make.
There's nothing to say about this loneliness.
At least this comfort between us, teacups
and the kitchen temporarily warm.
It's snowing again, not without a kind of solace.
The light is liquid and holding; the river,
stuck into a white sheet, is a non-ending
silent road to itself.

Meditation on Crete

No one talks on this old island.
You'll see them with their nets
under the endless clumps of olive
and never notice the cypress pine,
ancient water trees that reach through rock
to grow up here. Not even the barren pray
on the roadside to the dusty crosses in glass.
Everything is understood in this language.

It's not the steep road that stops me
from going down to the sea. Here
they know one glimpse of that color
can blind the eye of your own good sense,
a trick in the old days when sight was often cut away.
The gods were simple as those shells
washing the water brilliant.

I have learned it is better to walk in this dust,
why you must cover your head
here on the mountain. The women keep themselves
in black. I have come back to them,
counting my losses like children
until there is nothing left but regret.
It flies to the center of my body
as the gods meant it when they gave us fire.

When I watch the feathery silver of the morning
clouds rising from the sea, the silver
black pods on that knotted carob,
I imagine the man who saw them as he built the wings
he would fly on out of this place.
To think a man's arms could carry him,
to think the gods would allow his own son
freedom from the bounds of salt spray and sun.

These are the stories you will hear
until they find your life, until greed falls away
and you ask nothing. Up here on the mountain,
I understand the one who could pass the silver thread
through the tiniest spiraled shell,
how nothing was left but to wrap iron bands
about his heart, lest it break with grief.

IV. For Bill

Your Mother Takes Us Back to Liberty

Both of you have come sadly to walk the land.
I've never seen so much stone,
a creekbed filled with vines.
I wear Sunday best, your mother vague in silver.
You're dressed for this country: your boots are black.
The car drags sumac in its pipes.

We drive up the green mountain,
past the empty cabins, the aunts and uncles
hardly more silent than all the days they sat
in the twilight after the same meal,
after boiling the clothes in the same black pot.
You take the car as far as it will go
on the re-claimed road. We trample wild lilies
to Wilbur's cabin. Five years and the wilderness
grows over like a grave. Up here, a man owns
what he owns until the hills take it back.
Under dust, a knife and fork laid for supper,
behind the shredded closet curtain,
his lumber coat still hangs. Nothing moves
but your mother's brittle voice.

I can't understand one empty house
after another, this silence and how each landmark
has held its ground these thirty years.
You do not help your reed-thin mother
pick through the stones. She holds a fist
of tiger lilies, goes half a century back
to gingham, walking the wagon road to Reliance
in curls that match your own, the face that is your face.

I'd rather think about the blackberries
filling the creek, Drucilla's pasture;
waist-deep and red. A week too early for the best,
still I tuck my skirt and wade in. I refuse you
when you call, fill your mother's bonnet full.
You take a cornerstone from your grandfather's cabin.

You tell me again: here is the latch,
the pegged door-latch, and here is the same moon
rising over the chimney, the light
as flimsy and thin. And this is the stone
that looked like a face, the same face
you watched behind gauze as everyone slept.

We go further back on the mountain
to search where there is nothing,
save shattered roads and a rebuilt church.
Where I see nothing, you tell me
it is all still there: hard evidence
you find in rotted dovetails, rock hearth.
And where they worshipped, a place to lay the dead.
They lie pressed to the body of the earth
which does not know the difference.
Once lined in rows of bellflower, the stones crumble.
You step back into kudzu, that fierce green
which has grown up thicker than you remember,
holding you there as it twists among the graves.

You Go Home, 1968

1. Briar Creek

He walked you around on his land
all afternoon, khaki shirt stuck to your back.
Pointed out blackberries, gave you walnuts
impossible to crack. Talking to him
never changes: you can't get a word in.
He drove off in the Jewel Tea truck when you were five,
said he had to get back to the land,
those watery muskmelons, a new woman
and her snake-handling religion. His other kids
run around half wild. You don't ask why he left,
you still come see your father.
You'd like to walk to the west, to Briar Creek
where tenderfooted you waded once in underwear
three miles through stone and briar to Clinch River.

When the moon finds the yellow clouds
over Chilhowee Ridge, your father brings out pictures
a hundred years old: great-grandfather in uniform
and the one you were named for. He carved the bed
in the next room and wrote at your birth:
Wright, I've got five pigs put aside for you.
I'm proud of the new boy, help him carry the name.

2. Knoxville

At your mother's frame house
the twin apple trees bloom white. Stars
she called those flowers. There were nights
blossoms clung to the screen and the rain
couldn't keep you in; the train shook the porch
where you slept. That track went straight
to Cincinnati, where people were rich.
You repeated *Cincinnati* under your breath.

Under stars all the way to Knoxville,
you think about the summers your mother took you
to Aunt Dru's place. That garden's back to rock;
the cabin, washpot, lost in green.
They've strung electricity through the valley.
But the land takes back everything: black river bottom,
moccasin, wild plum. Men go crazy
trying to live in those hills. You know you won't go back,
though you've never seen a mist so fine
in the silver dusk, or any clouds as blue
burning off the stepped layers of Liberty Ridge.

Aunt Drucilla's Pasture

The cabin leans on the side of the hill,
brown as bark, gray as the willow
that drags the empty creek.
All paths lead to kudzu: kudzu
over the chimney, over the good black pot.

Empty country, except for Copper Hill.
Prisoner and quarry—each existed for the other.
Every summer you watched for them: murderers
in their gray and white overalls,
and went to sleep dreaming their evil crimes,
how they took away what belonged and was good.

The still hot day the warning whistle screamed
Dru was stirring the clothes with a maple stick.
Truckloads of men rode past, the guards
rode past. Dru spread the clothes on chinaberry
and went down to the field to hoe the corn.

You still see it: how the flock of crows
scattered like poppyseed on Liberty Ridge,
out of the clump of shagbark and waist-high laurel.
How Drucilla straightened and raised her hand
to bonnet rim, looked hard at the interrupted green,
how she went back to the hoeing.

V. In Another Life

In Another Life

A gray-black house of wooden slats
held up by air: will and air.
The upstairs veranda steadied the swaying
like a hand. The second floor shook,
every board shook, and whatever beings
walked that place loosened and stroked
the braid of my hair. Husband of my other life,
over and over you led me there.
Outside in the long grass, I trembled
seeing the transparent walls,
what emptiness held the beams. The faces
looked out as if they were my own.
Finally I went to live there, knowing you believed
I should go forward into those lives.
Look, you said, how the veranda will keep you safe:
the stream of stars that never move above it,
the fixed shadow of the trees.
You never saw how thin the wood was,
how I was given to those of my own kind
who laid over me their naked light
as I took from myself skin and bone.
You never guessed how easily I slipped
between the boards, between floors.

Bees

Mad with venom, they flew between the layers,
revealing the crevices in the brick.
I woke to the fine instrument of their hum
prisoned in the heart of the house.
Why had I disturbed the hive they wove from themselves,
sprayed poison in the tight nest over the door?
They dragged the egg sack into the darkness of my wall.
Even the crippled hatched; hundreds
crept out, struggled to fly.

I tried to live with the bees
as I have in my flawed house, tried to ignore
the ragged black mole in the center of my back.
But they had come to stay, half-sisters
nagging at my body, and that singing:
they broke my silence to die.

They beat on the windows and fell on the burning stove.
Open screen, open door—nothing took the smell.
Every morning I stomped the buzzing
along the floor. My bare feet found their litter,
found the dead ones with their tiny stings;
their song forced the closed space of my lungs.
                    The bees hammer at my house.
They leap in the walls to divide and die,
to leave the honeycomb, full and rich and deadly.

Delta House

My sister does not dream of drowning
or wake to measure the airport beam
that circled our small night sky,
the light steady enough to keep us,
growing up through water.
Summers the cypress sank deeper,
crop-sprayers woke us over the muddy cane.
The cotton soaked to ruin
in the river-heart of the delta.

We as children could not imagine the sea,
knew the rain's predictable silence.
The grass too wet to cut got higher.
Papou died and three times
they tried to dig his grave
it filled. His garden swelled,
left little to pick. Those nights
my sister clawed me awake,
looking for ground, the bottom
of the delta. Or curled into herself so still
I knew the water had filled her lungs
at last. I kept to my side.

My sister has a new house, lives alone.
From her window she looks down
on the measured ocean, preferring height,
an absence of green. She loves salt
drying the air, moves her hands through sand.
Though I don't know her house,
the rock where it rests, the division
of water and land. We do not talk
from our separate places.
Someday I'll visit and we'll say this
against the explicit background of the sea.

Peaches: For My Mother

I should have brought you to these trees
where I'm pulling Red-kist peaches. It's sunset
and I hand them down to your mother
who expects the best for the basket. She tells me
to climb higher. Up here in this light,
everything's the same, how my grandmother
holds her hand against the light to guide me,
the yellow jam she'll make. She motions
for the ripest, wants the peaches I can't reach.
The trees are old, laced with briars.

                        I could be ten
with braids, barefoot. I've always climbed
this way, though silks of hair hang on limbs
and my scratched arms sting. If you were here,
the picking would take twice as long.
Eating and talking, you'd stumble around
on your bad leg, nervous I would fall.

I'd show you how to choose the fruit: smooth cream
and blush of red. Then watch you pick the ones
hanging lowest, with a greenish cast or streaks
of tree tar. You'd rub your knee,
insist it didn't hurt. And breaking peaches,
marvel at this light, the pitch black
of peaches still perfect on the limb. You'd wonder
if there's a painting like that.

We allow so little to one another.
I'm held on this high branch
as another day folds down. My grandmother will break
with the certainty of the old. Walking from this field
she won't let me take her hand. And you, Mama,
whom I have not preferred,
I have thought of all this time.

Snow

How the snow goes on
until you wake to something you've never known,
where no one is weeping. The silence

finds itself, the landscape
calling you to pay attention
to whatever is in your eye, maybe your life
looks different in this light. Movement
proves what can be broken: that calm
of white across the yard, ice
or the limb's crack underfoot.
And called by the plunge of snow
from the fir outside your window,
you'll find the ring around the streetlight
or the moon, the cobwebs of ice
making a tunnel through the light.
This is all accidental. You'll see
how it moves toward reconciliation.
You will go for long walks in the snow.

Foreigner

I find you in this country
where field finds marsh,
where land deceives the eye.
You come as fisherman,
knee-deep in the brackish water.
Birds rest on you, limb,
pine-stalk that you are,
and I can't understand your arrival,
how you find your balance
in water whose limits you cannot know.
You are wearing risk
as if it were a knotted scarf.
I wear a fish around my neck,
it falls away like a heart
or anything that is needed or given.

You have told me how the snow
before it falls, hovers like a white mass
confining the air beneath,
and you must only look up to see it
waiting, to know the certainty
with which it will cover you.
I began to see for the first time
your thin shoulder blades under flannel
and hidden, the scarred bone of your skull.
I saw you walking as though
you accepted any loneliness,
as though a blizzard were a small thing.

We trade these landscapes.
Mine, the same uncertain land,
that haze of water given to water
collects in my footsteps.
Yours is white and bare,
marked by line, clear as the crossing
veins of my wrists. I am walking
through the flawed light of the snow.
There is the clean definition of a creek
that travels this immense field,
the ice holding the water, and you
walk toward me as though it were no distance.
Brother of my hunger, in this dream
we lie down on the familiar body of the earth.

Journey in the Snow Season

1.

They are trying to make you safe
in the white bed, in the white room.
Heart, you think, webbed pattern
of crosses, how the flesh performs
its good rituals. But nothing stops this blood
from flowing: again it passes
the soft packets of tissue. Painless
you begin to say, though the gripped circle
of your waist is wrung and wrung.

2.

You have been looking at your hands.
They are like guests, removed and private.
You can't explain your life
but think of the ducks fluttering in the park
late at night, across from your own room,
wild rabbits taking lettuce by the fence.
You remember one night the reindeer in their pen charged
and shook their antlers against the ice
as if it were spring. Turning on themselves
they fought until dawn.
Over and over you've watched the animals
live out their lives. The earth takes in water
or blood, whatever falls.

3.

A veil of snow slides from a branch,
the particles of light fly out
and disappear. A yearling raises its stumpy antlers
and begins to dance, stirring the others
to rise and race across the pond.

You have loved your body for the wrong reasons.
How capable it is, and vain: it loves to walk
and lie down. Imagine the tiny roads
drawing into the heart, a house
visible through thin ribbed trees.
When the snow begins, you are resting in that net
of branches. By now the deer will be perfectly still,
their noses lifted in the first snow.

The Animals Choose Their Path into My Sleep

I had given them up in that place,
abandoned the old path that rose secretly
out of the sodden ground, avoided the moon
which also rose from water. Each night in a curse
I stumbled there. I thought it was the old sweet taste
in my mouth, my greedy promises that kept them away.
Every night I washed the dark smell
from my body, called for them to bless me
with their peace, their senseless beauty.
I was not watching when the two deer
leaped across the road, their eyes furious
as they disappeared into the usual haze of rain.

I knew the animals had come back into my sleep,
into the pine fields caked with red clay.
I claimed it all: went back to swamp,
wrapped-cypress; left mother and father,
gave back the helpless disguise I had stripped
from them, the stinging garment.
Took the knife and the flesh it severed
from hide or fin, took the water I'd refused,
fists of clay.

I found another marsh-field, my own reflection
in a cranberry bog. Pink blossoms fell
on my wrists, the net of red berries in my hand.
And the cranes came, namesake to that marsh
for centuries, making their return
out of this dark world. Purely white
they rested there, and I among them
whom they recognized. Yet they chose to stay
and reveal themselves, baring their perfect necks,
the delicate canopy of wings. And I thought
what line they follow over this earth,
what simple navigation, while I have cried out
need and blame, searching every broken path.

Cleopatra Mathis

Half-Greek and part Cherokee Indian, Cleopatra Mathis was born in Ruston, Louisiana in 1947. She attended Tulane University, where she received a B.A. in English. After teaching in Texas for five years, she moved to New Jersey. She received an M.F.A. in writing from Columbia University in 1978. Presently, she is working in the Poetry in Schools program in New Jersey. She is married, and has a daughter, Alexandra.